Amazing Nature

Hidden Hibernators

Malcolm Penny

Heinemann Library
Chicago, Illinois

Produced for Heinemann Library by Discovery Books Limited
Originated by Ambassador Litho Ltd
Printed in China by South China Printing Company

08 07 06 05 04
10 9 8 7 6 5 4 3 2 1

Library of Congress Cataloging-in-Publication Data
Penny, Malcolm.
  Hidden hibernators / Malcolm Penny.
      p. cm. -- (Amazing nature)
Summary: Describes the ways animals hibernate during the winter,
explaining the difference between true hibernators and light sleepers,
and how they wake up in the spring.
Includes bibliographical references (p.   ) and index.
  ISBN 1-4034-4704-7 (Hardcover) -- ISBN 1-4034-5400-0 (pbk.)
  1. Hibernation--Juvenile literature. [1. Hibernation. 2.
Animals--Wintering.] I. Title. II. Series.
  QL755.P46 2003
  591.56'5--dc22

                              2003022040

Acknowledgments
The publisher would like to thank the following for permission to reproduce photographs:
p. 4 Richard Packwood/Oxford Scientific Films; p. 5 Breck P. Kent/AA/Oxford Scientific Films; p. 7 Kim Taylor/Bruce Coleman Collection; p. 8 Claude Steelman/Survival Anglia/Oxford Scientific Films; p. 9 Andrew Purcell/Bruce Coleman Collection; p. 10 Breck P. Kent/AA/Oxford Scientific Films; p. 11 John Shaw/Bruce Coleman Collection; p. 12 Daniel Heuclin/Natural History Photographic Agency; p. 13 Tom Ulrich/Oxford Scientific Films; p. 14A Daniel Heuclin/Natural History Photographic Agency; p. 14B Zig Leszczynski/AA/Oxford Scientific Films; p. 15 Bill Wood/Natural History Photographic Agency; p. 16A Richard Packwood/Oxford Scientific Films; p. 16B Mike Linley/Oxford Scientific Films; p. 17 Daniel Heuclin/Natural History Photographic Agency; p. 18 G. I. Bernard/Natural History Photographic Agency; p. 19 David Hosking/FLPA; p. 20 Stephen Dalton/Natural History Photographic Agency; p. 21 Frirz Polking/FLPA; p. 22 Des & Jen Bartlett/SAL/Oxford Scientific Films; p. 23 Daniel Heuclin/Natural History Photographic Agency; p. 24A Eric Soder/Natural History Photographic Agency; p. 24B Professor Jack Dermid/Oxford Scientific Films; p. 25 Martin Harvey/Natural History Photographic Agency; p. 26 T. Kitchen & V. Hurst/Natural History Photographic Agency; p. 27 Daniel Cox/Oxford Scientific Films; p. 28 M. Hoshino/Minden Pictures/FLPA; p. 29 Joe McDonald/Bruce Coleman Collection.

Cover photograph of an eastern chipmunk: Breck P. Kent/AA/Oxford Scientific Films.

Every effort has been made to contact copyright holders of any material reproduced in this book. Any omissions will be rectified in subsequent printings if notice is given to the publisher.

Some words are shown in bold, **like this.** You can find out what they mean by looking in the glossary.

Contents

What Is a Hibernator?

The winter is a very difficult time for animals. It can be very cold. Snow may cover the ground, making food hard to find. Some animals have **adapted** to cope with these conditions. Others travel to warmer places.

But many animals spend the winter months asleep. This sleep is called **hibernation,** which means "wintering." The animals that hibernate are called hibernators. One of these hibernators, the Arctic ground squirrel, hibernates for eight months of the year, from October to May. It spends more than half of its life asleep!

A hibernating animal is not just asleep. It is very cold, it hardly breathes, and its heart beats very slowly. It does not need to feed while it is hibernating, because it is using very little **energy.**

This hibernating lesser horseshoe bat is covered in dewdrops. Here, in an old mine, the temperature will not change very much through the winter.

Different kinds of animals start hibernating in different ways. Some go right to sleep, while others go through a drowsy time first. But they all wake up in much the same way, gradually waking from their deep slumber as spring returns.

Just resting

Not all animals that take a long rest during the winter are real hibernators. Some of them are just sleeping. These animals are called **shallow hibernators**. They are not much colder than usual, they breathe normally, and their heart beats slowly, just as it does in all sleeping animals. Shallow hibernators do not save as much energy as the really deep sleepers.

An eastern chipmunk does not awake from hibernation even when the leaves covering it are gently moved away.

Deep Sleepers

Mammals are warm-blooded. This means that they can make their own body heat, even in cold weather. To do this, they turn the food they eat into heat. Only three groups of mammals truly **hibernate**. These are the **rodents** (animals such as rats, mice, hamsters, and ground squirrels), the **insectivores** (a group of **insect**-eaters that includes hedgehogs), and bats. Only one kind of bird is a hibernator, an insect-eater called the poorwill.

Reptiles, such as snakes and lizards, and **amphibians,** such as frogs, toads, and salamanders, are called cold-blooded. This is because they cannot make their own body heat. Their bodies only work properly when they are warmed up by spring and summer weather. These animals need to hibernate because they cannot hunt for food in cold weather. Even if they could find food, their bodies could not **digest** it.

Barely alive

A human's body temperature stays the same whether he or she is awake or asleep. The rate at which the human heart beats is almost the same whether resting or sleeping. Hibernating mammals, however, become like cold-blooded animals. Their body temperature falls until it is the same as the air around them.

When a ground squirrel is hibernating, it breathes only about three times each minute, and its heart beats about once a minute. Its temperature falls from 100.4 °F (38 °C) to 32 °F (0 °C). Its blood stops flowing through its legs and the back part of its body. Blood only flows to keep its heart muscle working and to allow **oxygen** to reach its brain.

The name of the dormouse means "the mouse that sleeps." While it hibernates, its store of fat keeps it alive.

Sleepy Bears and Hedgehogs

Bears sleep through the winter, but they are **shallow hibernators**. Their body temperature only falls by about 39 °F (4 °C). Brown (grizzly) bears and black bears spend the winter in an underground **den**. Brown bears usually dig out a hole in a hillside, often under the roots of a large tree. Black bears prefer hollow trees or small caves. Both kinds of bears will sometimes sleep under piles of logs or tree branches. While they are in their den, bears doze most of the time, but they do not fall deeply asleep. This means they can wake up properly in only a few minutes.

Black bear mothers like this one sleep with their cubs in their winter dens. During warm winters, some black bears only sleep for two or three weeks.

Born in winter

Brown bears living in the cold, far north of North America can sleep for seven months of the year. Black bears living much further south, where it is warmer, only sleep for a few weeks. Bears wake up from time to time during the winter but they do not eat. Females give birth to their cubs in the den, and nurse them as they sleep. By the time spring comes, the cubs are well grown and active.

Sleeping and feeding

Other shallow hibernators are chipmunks in North America and hedgehogs in Europe, Asia, and Africa. Chipmunks wake regularly to eat food that they have stored in their burrows. On mild winter days, European hedgehogs actually go outside to feed, and then go back to sleep again. In hard winters, hedgehogs can behave like deep hibernators, and stay asleep for several months.

Hedgehogs help gardeners by eating plant-loving slugs and snails. This hedgehog has hibernated in a pile of dead leaves under a garden hedge.

Getting Ready for Bed

Inthe fall, animals get ready to take shelter from the winter. The first sign that winter is coming is the lack of daylight, not the cooler weather. As the sun sets earlier every day, animals know that the time to find shelter is coming. **Shallow hibernators** must store food in their burrows or in their stomachs and find a way to keep warm.

Brown bears in Alaska roam the hillsides, feeding on fruits and berries. They also look for a good place to dig their **dens**. In North America, chipmunks gather food to store in their burrows. Hedgehogs in Europe take leaves and dry grass to a sheltered place before snuggling into them to keep warm.

An eastern chipmunk collects fruits and nuts to snack on during the winter.

A hoary marmot in Alaska gathers bedding to line its den for the family's winter sleep.

Snuggling up

Marmots are large **rodents** related to squirrels. They live in Europe, Canada, and Alaska. The entire marmot family group, which may have as many as fifteen animals, huddles together in its den for as long as six months. The last one to creep in, usually an adult male, blocks the entrance from the inside using dry grass and dirt.

Time for sleep

Animals go to sleep at different speeds. Golden hamsters put up with the cold for as long as three months before falling asleep, while pocket mice hibernate at once after only a few days of cold weather.

Hiding on Land

Hibernators must find a safe place where they will not be found by animals that might eat them. Some hibernators dig holes to hide in. Others look for already-made holes or seek out cracks in rocks and hollow trees. Small reptiles and amphibians may creep into woodpiles or holes in fallen logs. Or, they may hide under stones or dead leaves on the forest floor.

This common toad has found a mossy hole under a bank to hide in while it hibernates.

The colocolo is a small **marsupial mammal** that lives in Chile. It hibernates in a waterproof nest that it builds from bamboo leaves. The nest is wedged into a hole in a tree or inside a rotten log. The colocolo lines the inside with dry grass or moss. It eats a lot during the summer, then survives the winter by living on fat that is stored around the base of its tail.

Slowing down

Only one bird, the poorwill, hibernates. The poorwill is an American member of the nightjar family. Nightjars are a group of **insect**-eating birds found all over the world. Most insect-eating birds **migrate** to warmer places or change their diet in winter, but poorwills just creep into one of their favorite hollows in a rock and cool down to become almost as cold as the winter air. Their **digestion,** heartbeat and breathing all slow down, until they wake in the spring.

A poorwill waits for sunset, when it can start catching insects to eat. In winter, it will hide away to hibernate.

13

Hiding under Water

Most turtles **hibernate** by burrowing into the mud at the bottom of a pool of water. They stay there for the whole winter, even when the water is covered in ice. Because turtles breathe so slowly, they can survive with only the air that is trapped in their shells. Salamanders, toads, and other **amphibians** burrow into the mud at the bottom of a pool of water before falling into a deep sleep until warmer weather returns.

In summer, a red-eared slider basks in the warm sunshine before slipping into the water to feed.

Turtle and tortoise links

A turtle called the red-eared slider lives in the southern United States and northern South America. It hibernates on land like a tortoise, instead of under water like other turtles. When the weather starts to cool down, it looks for an empty muskrat burrow, or maybe a hollow log, in which to spend the winter.

This gopher tortoise is at the entrance to its burrow in a sandy bank. In winter, it will hibernate deep inside.

Broken homes

Very few fish hibernate, but the toadfish does. It gets it name from its wide mouth, and because it makes a croaking noise when it is caught. Toadfish are common along the east coast of North America. They make their nests on the seabed. At one time, they nested in large, empty shells or holes in rocks, but now they usually nest in tin cans and broken bottles, and even in old shoes! Toadfish can live out of water for many hours, but during the winter, when worms and crabs are hard to find, they hibernate buried in mud at the bottom of the sea.

A banded toadfish lurks in a burrow in the seabed. It is covered in whiskery tufts, which make it harder to see.

Sleeping in Groups

Most bats that live in cooler parts of the world **hibernate** in damp caves or in hollow trees during the winter. Sometimes they gather in barns or church towers, usually in a group in the roof. Huddling together helps them to survive in two ways. First, it keeps them a little warmer than they would be if they were hanging up alone. Second, it keeps them from becoming too dry. The water in their skins will **evaporate** more slowly when they are surrounded by other bats' bodies rather than when they are surrounded by air.

A cluster of lesser horseshoe bats hibernates on the ceiling of an old mine. In this damp cavern, they are in no danger of drying out.

Bat links

The Mexican freetail bat does not hibernate. Instead, when winter comes it **migrates** 992 miles (1,600 km) from the United States to Mexico, where it is warmer.

Mexican freetail bats huddle together in a Texas cave to keep warm even on summer days. In winter, they will be gone.

Northern Pacific rattlesnakes spend the winter sleeping close together in a deep, dark cave.

Cozy caves

Snakes live alone most of the time, but when winter comes they often group together. In Canada, thousands of red-sided garter snakes make their way into caves where they hibernate for seven months of the year. In the northern United States rattlesnakes gather in holes and caves to sleep through the winter. The swift-moving snakes called racers that live in Europe, Asia, and the United States also hibernate in crowds.

The snakes seek each other out and crowd together, often winding themselves around each other. No one is quite sure why snakes hibernate together. Perhaps, like bats, it keeps them a little warmer than if they were alone. Some caves seem to be better than others for hibernating, but we do not yet know why. When the outside air begins to warm up as spring approaches, both snakes and bats can feel the change, and they begin to wake up.

Sleepy Creepy-Crawlies

Most **insects** die in the winter. Only their eggs or **pupae** survive, because they do not need to feed. The new adults emerge in spring. But there are some insects that **hibernate** as adults.

A queen wasp hibernates hanging upside down from a twig deep inside a thick hedge, clinging on with her feet and jaws.

Wasps live in large, busy groups during the summer. There may be thousands of workers collecting food and tending the young in the nest. Wasps mainly eat other insects, and they cannot store food. When winter comes and there are no insects to hunt, all the workers die. Only the adult queens survive. They do so by hibernating in some sheltered corner, like a crack in the bark of a tree, under a pile of dead leaves, or in a house. All through the summer they have been eating as much food as they can find to build up a store of fat. Their blood changes as winter comes along, making a chemical that stops their blood from freezing.

Holed up

Some bees that live alone survive in a different way. In summer, the females make nests in holes. They leave their eggs with a store of **pollen** and **nectar** for the **larvae** to eat when they hatch. Then the females all die. Their young hibernate in their burrows as pupae, ready to emerge as adults in the spring. Only honey bees survive the winter without hibernating, because they can store honey and pollen to eat through the winter.

Adult mason bees die before the winter, leaving their young to hibernate. Soon this young mason bee will dig a hole in which she will leave her eggs.

The Big Switch-off

Most butterflies survive the winter as **pupae,** but some kinds **hibernate** as adults. These are mostly tortoiseshells or peacock butterflies. In the wild, they hibernate in hollow trees or in cracks in rocks. Many make their way into houses, where they find a cosy sleeping place. Hibernating butterflies can be in trouble in warm houses. If they wake from their winter sleep when there are no flowers where they can find **nectar,** they will starve.

Peacock butterflies often hibernate behind furniture, or, as seen here, in the folds of a curtain.

An American butterfly, the monarch, travels before it hibernates. In summer some of them live in California and some in Canada, but when winter approaches they all fly south to Mexico. There, they hibernate in huge groups as they hang in pine forest trees.

Like orange flowers covering the trees, millions of monarch butterflies hibernate in pine trees in the highlands of Mexico.

Slowing down

All these butterflies, and many **insects,** can stop producing the chemicals that control their growth. This makes their bodies slow down. Scientists call this clever trick **diapause,** which means "waiting time." The insect's body loses water, and just before diapause starts many insects build up a store of fat to keep them alive. Insects usually switch to diapause when the weather is too cold, but also when it is too hot or dry. We now know that other animals, such as snails, can do it, too. When conditions improve, the animals can switch on again, and continue their lives as if nothing had happened.

A Waterproof Coat

In hot countries, some animals escape from long, dry periods by hiding. Hiding from hot weather is called **estivation,** which means "summering." As they dry out, some estivators become covered in dried-up **mucus** like a thick, plastic bag.

The African bullfrog lives in the usually damp river valleys and woodlands in east and central Africa. When the long, dry season is about to start, the bullfrog digs a burrow while the ground is still soft. When it is underground, it spreads mucus over its body with its front and back feet. The frog then goes to sleep, and the mucus dries. Weeks or months later, when the first rain seeps into the ground, the mucus coating softens and the frog wakes up. It peels the mucus off its skin, and eats it. Then it digs its way out into the air.

Wrapped up until the rains return, an African bullfrog is covered in a coating of dried mucus. This one has been carefully dug out of its burrow.

This African lungfish in Cameroon was dug up by a jackal. Its leathery estivation coat is cracked, so the lungfish will not survive.

Taking a breather

Another group of estivators are the lungfish, which are found in pools of freshwater in warm parts of Africa, Australia, and South America. They are called lungfish because they breathe through their mouths, using lungs, not gills like other fish. When dry weather comes, and the water level in a pool of water falls, a lungfish burrows tail first into the soft mud at the bottom. If it did not do this and the pool dried up altogether, the lungfish would die. A lungfish is always covered in slimy mucus, which hardens as it dries into a waterproof coat. The only opening is a narrow tube leading up the hole the fish made as it burrowed. It uses this to breathe. A lungfish can wait for up to four years for rain to fall.

Waiting for the Rain

Some of the most amazing **estivators** are the **larvae** of African mosquitoes that live in the dry region south of the Sahara Desert. They can survive by drying up completely, until they are just like grains of sand. They blow about on the floor of the desert until the rains return, or until they are blown into a pool of water. When they have soaked up some water they come back to life, sometimes many years later. They turn into **pupae** and then into adults, and fly off looking for food.

A fire salamander that lives in Switzerland has to hibernate to survive the freezing Alpine winter.

Salamander links

Salamanders that live in warm countries survive hot weather by estivating, while, in cooler countries, salamanders **hibernate.**

A lesser siren is a salamander that lives in streams in North Carolina. If the stream dries up, it will have to estivate.

Crocodiles like to bask in the African sun, but they have a hole ready in the riverbank in case the weather gets too dry.

Too hot to move

Crocodiles are cold-blooded **reptiles** that cannot control their body temperature. Those that live in warmer places estivate during dry periods. In very hot, dry conditions, crocodiles have to take cover. They do it by hiding in a tunnel or cave in the bank of the river where they live, or by burying themselves in the mud beside a stream. Sometimes they get into any shallow pools that are left, where they lie still just below the surface with only their nostrils showing. They become slow and sluggish, and hardly feed at all.

When wetter conditions finally return, estivating animals wake up. They have survived the weather that would otherwise have killed them, and they are hungry and eager to carry on with their normal lives.

Wake-Up Time

When spring comes, **hibernating mammals** wake up. But what tells them when to wake? It seems that either they can sense the slight rise in temperature as the weather warms up, or else the chemical in their brain that keeps them asleep is running out. Hibernating mammals wake up very gradually. Their narrow blood vessels—the tubes that carry the blood around the body—must get wider slowly. If they all opened up at once, the animal's **blood pressure** would fall suddenly, and it might die.

The first parts to warm up are the head and the heart, which both kept a tiny blood supply during hibernation. When those are warm, the rest of the front of the body comes to life. The middle of the body, and then finally the back legs, follow.

Soon after it wakes up in spring, an Arctic ground squirrel will line its burrow again, this time to raise a family.

*These brown bear cubs in Montana were born in their mother's **den** during the winter.*

Hibernation saves **energy,** but a hibernator must use up some stored food to stay alive. Some animals lose nearly half their body weight while they hibernate. **Shallow hibernators** that wake up during the winter lose the most weight, because they have to burn energy to move. Those that store food in their sleeping nests do best, because they can feed indoors without wasting energy by going outside.

Hibernation is a risky business, and many animals do not wake up from their long sleep. Hibernators are very rarely found by predators, though, because they are so well hidden.

Fact File

Hibernators can survive being very cold for long periods, but their **parasites** cannot. During the summer, bats suffer from a type of worm in their stomach. But in winter, all the worms die. Skin parasites like ticks and mites also die from cold while animals hibernate.

Hibernating animals must be able to raise their young quickly, so that they and their young are ready to hibernate when winter comes. Arctic ground squirrels wake up in early May, **mate** two weeks later, and produce their young after 25 days, in mid-June. By the time they hibernate in late September or early October, the young are the same weight as the adults.

While an animal is hibernating, its muscles become weak. Many other parts of the body, including those that **digest** food, are damaged by not being used. Scientists studying ground squirrels find that everything has been repaired only 24 hours after the squirrel has woken up.

When a woodchuck starts to hibernate, its pulse falls from 153 to 68 beats per minute in the first half hour.

Some hibernating ground squirrels, including the Arctic and the long-clawed ground squirrels, will **estivate** during dry weather when their food plants are dry and not good to eat.

Hibernating Siberian chipmunks store seeds, acorns, mushrooms, and the buds of flowers in separate holes dug into the walls of their sleeping burrow.

Hibernating bats can survive very cold conditions. The coldest bat ever found was a red bat in North America, still alive at –58 °F (–50 °C).

A hibernating California ground squirrel's heart beats just once per minute. It has a body temperature of 41 °F (5 °C).

Glossary

adapt   to change in a way that better suits an animal to its surroundings

amphibian   animal that may live on land but must spend part of its life in the water

blood pressure   pressure inside blood vessels caused by the pumping of the heart

den   hole in which an animal lives or hibernates

diapause   period when an insect's life comes to a temporary stop

digest   turn food that has been eaten into a form that the body can use

energy   strength produced by using up food

estivate   to sleep deeply through the summer

evaporate   to turn from a liquid into a vapor

hibernate   to sleep deeply through the winter

insect   animal with six legs and three body parts: head, thorax, and abdomen

insectivore   insect-eating mammal such as a hedgehog or shrew

larva (more than one are called larvae)   stage in an insect's life after it hatches from the egg

mammal   warm-blooded, furry animal that feeds its young on milk produced by the mother

marsupial   mammal that carries its young in a pouch

mate   to mix male and female cells to create young

migrate   to travel regularly between two places as the seasons or living conditions change

mucus   slime produced by an animal

nectar   sugary liquid produced by flowers

oxygen   gas in the air that all living things need

parasite   creature that feeds on other living things while they are still alive

pollen   tiny, dust-like grains from the male part of a flower

pupa (more than one are called pupae)   stage in an insect's life between larva and adult

reptile   scaly animal such as a snake or a lizard

rodent   mammal with ever-growing front teeth that are used to gnaw hard food

shallow hibernator   animal that sleeps in winter but does not slow down its body as much as a hibernator does

more Books to Read

Fredericks, Anthony D. and Sneed B. Collard. *Amazing Animals: Nature's Most Incredible Creatures.* Chanhassen, Minn.: Creative Publishing International, 2000.

Kalman, Bobbie. *How Do Animals Adapt?* New York: Crabtree Publishing, 2000.

Kalman, Bobbie. *What Is Hibernation?* New York: Crabtree Publishing, 2001.

Index